A Little Indian Cookbook

Rafi Fernandez

ILLUSTRATED BY JOHN FAZAKERLEY

Chronicle Books

First published in 1992 by
The Appletree Press Ltd,
7 James Street South, Belfast BT2 8DL.
Copyright © 1992 The Appletree Press, Ltd.
Illustrations © 1992 The Appletree Press, Ltd.
Printed in the E.C. All rights reserved.
No part of this publication may be reproduced
or transmitted in any form or by means,
electronic or mechanical, photocopying,
recording or any information and retrieval
system, without permission in writing from
the publisher.

A Little Indian Cookbook

First published in the United States in 1992 by
Chronicle Books, 275 Fifth Street,
San Francisco, CA 94103

ISBN: 0-8118-0265-5

9 8 7 6 5 4 3 2 1

Introduction

"Namaste", the catch-all phrase that means "hello", "goodbye", or even "how are you?", denotes gentle respect. The gesture of folded hands indicates the grace and welcome to be encountered all over India. The timeless mystery and beauty of India is 5,000 years old: a land peopled by a hundred races, speaking a hundred tongues. Give each the due of its own cultural and religious influences and let the centuries roll on. You will then get a rich profusion of eating habits, each a little different, each just a little more exotic. The unforgettable aroma of India is not just the heavy scent of jasmine and roses. It is also the fragrance of spices so important to Indian cooking. The word "curry" is an English derivative of *"kari"*, meaning spice sauce, and today, with Indians widely spread in western countries, there are some very good curry powders and pastes available in markets worldwide. These have been subtly blended with spices such as turmeric, cardamon, ginger, coriander, nutmeg, cinnamon, and many more. *"Bawarchis"*, or master chefs, have created infinite dishes using individual spices, like artists with a palette of colors. Surely no other country can lay before you such a diverse spectrum of foods or promise you a gastronomic adventure quite like India.

A note on measures

Spoon measurements are level except where otherwise indicated. Seasonings can of course be adjusted according to taste. Recipes are for four, unless otherwise noted.

The Modern Indian Kitchen

Today several commercial brands offer prepared *masalas* (blended spice mix) in powder and paste form, and I find these a great boon. Test different brands to find your preference.

Varieties of *masala* mixes

Kashmiri	Mild or hot curry
Green	Madras
Garam	Pasanda
Tikka	Bhuna
Tandoori	Roghan Josh
Kebab	Vindaloo
Biryani	Dhansak

Other useful pastes

If possible, obtain the following pastes in Indian or Chinese brands as they are pure with no additives. Once opened, they will keep in the refrigerator for up to three weeks or they can be divided into portions and frozen.

Ginger	Garlic
Coriander	Red or green chilli
Mixed ginger, garlic and green chilli	

Other ingredients

It is also possible to obtain commercial deep-fried onion, a great time saver, with 2oz equalling 1 large raw onion. Curry leaves *(Kariyapath)* and coriander leaves *(Kotmir)* are available, fresh or dried. (Fresh leaves can be washed, dried and open-frozen.)

Coconut milk (*Nariyal doodh*) is available in cans, powdered form, or in cream blocks. To obtain 6 fl oz thick coconut milk add 3oz coconut cream to 6 fl oz boiling water. To obtain 6 fl oz thin coconut milk, add 1 oz coconut cream to 6 fl oz boiling water.

Gram flour is flour made from split peas. *Gram* or *dhals* are pulses — red lentils, moong beans, and so on. The former is the whole grain seed and the latter come in split form and are sometimes washed and husked.

Khushka/Chawal

Plain Boiled Rice

Freshly-boiled rice is cooked daily all over India but is favored more in South India. Rice, the ancient sages of India believed, is a gift of the gods, and its preparation is a form of prayer.

---

1 1/2 cups Patna or Basmati rice
3 cups water
1 tsp butter, vegetable, or olive oil
1/2 tsp salt or to taste

Pick and wash the rice in several changes of water. Allow to soak for 30 minutes (if possible) for fluffier, cooked grains. Drain well and put the rice in a heavy pan which has a tight-fitting lid. Add the measured water, butter or oil, and salt. Bring to boil, turn the heat to very low, cover and simmer for 12–15 minutes. To serve, loosen the rice with a flat slotted spoon to release the steam and prevent damaging the grains.

Bhaghara Khushka (Pulao Rice)

First sauté the drained rice in butter or oil along with $1/2$ tsp black cumin seeds, 1 inch piece of cinnamon stick, 2 green cardamoms and 2 bay leaves. Add the water and salt and proceed as for plain boiled rice.

When the rice is cooked, lift the lid and pour the food color of your choice, mixed in a little milk, randomly on the surface of the rice. Cover the pan and rest for 5 minutes before serving as above. Garnish with browned onions and almond flakes.

Naan

Leavened Bread

The variety of Indian breads is infinite but the *naan* is by far the most popular one in the western world. Although, traditionally, they are baked in a *tandoor* (clay oven), they are just as delicious baked in an ordinary oven.

---

1 tsp sugar	1 tsp salt
1 tsp fresh or dried yeast	1 egg yolk beaten or
5 fl oz warm water	a little milk
8oz plain flour	2 tsp poppy/onion/sesame
3oz melted ghee *or*	seeds (or mixed)
unsalted butter	

Place the sugar, yeast and warm water in a cup. Whisk well and rest until it turns frothy. Sieve the flour and salt. Make a well and pour in the yeast mixture along with the *ghee* or butter. Mix together with your fingers. Now rub your palms with a little *ghee* or butter and make a smooth and soft dough. Knead for about 5 minutes. Cover and rest dough covered for

8

2 hours or more to rise. Divide into 6 portions and gently roll out on a lightly floured surface. Brush with egg or milk and sprinkle on the seeds. Place on greased baking tray and bake for 10–15 minutes in a preheated oven at 450°F. Serve immediately or keep warm wrapped in foil.

Gosht Biryani

Rice Layered with Meat

Id-ul-Fitr marks the end of the Ramazan fast at the appearance of the new moon. *Fitr* means 5 pounds of grain which is distributed to the poor. *Biryani* is truly a jewel made for a royal treat and therefore a favorite with the *Noobs* of Hyderabad. Served with Egg and Tomato Curry (p. 40) and a *raitha* (p. 12), it cannot fail to please.

5 fl oz milk	I tsp turmeric powder
I sachet saffron powder	salt to taste and I tsp sugar
6 tbsp lemon juice	2 lbs cubed lamb or boned
4 green chillies, finely chopped	chicken
4 oz fresh coriander, chopped	I lb Basmati rice
	I tsp black cumin seeds
5 fl oz natural yogurt, beaten	4 green cardamoms
	2 in cinnamon stick
4 tbsp biryani masala	6 tbsp melted ghee or unsalted
2 tbsp garam masala	butter

Mix the milk and saffron and keep aside. Mix the next 8 items and marinade the lamb or chicken in it for 4–6 hours. Gently simmer it for 45 minutes in a heavy pan. Meanwhile, wash the rice and cook with whole spices in boiling water until the grains are a quarter done. Drain.

Grease the base of a heavy pan and place half the rice in an even but loose layer. Spread the cooked meat mixture with all the juices over the rice. Spread the remaining rice over this in a loose neat layer. Pour the saffron milk over the rice at random spots. Finally pour the *ghee* or butter over the rice. Grease a circular piece of foil (the size of the pan) and place it greased side down on the rice. Cover the pan and cook on low to medium heat for about 20 minutes or until the rice is fluffy. Gently toss the rice and meat together before serving.

Raitha

Yogurt, Mint and Cucumber Salad

---

10 fl oz natural yogurt, beaten
2 tsp mint sauce (or to taste)
salt and sugar to taste
4oz cucumber, thinly sliced
1/2 tsp paprika
fresh mint leaves for garnish

Mix the yogurt, sauce, salt, sugar, and cucumber gently together and chill. Garnish with paprika and mint leaves and serve.

Roghan Josh

Lamb in a Deep Red Sauce

A visit to Kashmir is incomplete until you have stayed on a houseboat on the beautiful Dal lake and eaten meals cooked by the *khansaba* (cook) on the kitchen boat which travels alongside the main houseboat.

1 tbsp ghee *or* vegetable oil	8–10 saffron strands *or*
1/2 tsp asafoetida powder	1 sachet powdered saffron
1 lb cubed lean lamb	1/2 tsp sugar
5 fl oz natural yogurt	salt to taste
beaten with 1/2 tsp cornstarch	4 tbsp tomato purée
2 tbsp roghan josh	blanched almond flakes
1 tsp kashmiri masala	for garnish
1 tsp garam masala	

Heat the *ghee* or oil in a heavy pan and fry the asafoetida and lamb on a medium heat until the meat pieces are sealed. Remove from the heat and cool a little. Fold in the yogurt and return to the heat and cook until the yogurt is absorbed. Add the remaining ingredients except the garnish and cook until the meat is tender and the gravy almost dry. Garnish with the almond flakes and serve hot. If you prefer a hotter curry *(phaal)*, then add 2 tsp chilli powder with the *masalas* to the above recipe and you will achieve the hottest curry available in restaurants.

Rafi's Paretal

Dry Meat Curry

This recipe is dedicated to all my pupils who love it, especially Peter who made double batches in his wok that looked like a volcano erupting. It is truly a "Rafi" invention for those who like it hot.

---

1 1/2 tsp chilli powder (or adjust to taste)
2 tbsp madras curry powder
1 tsp turmeric powder
salt to taste
3 tbsp vegetable oil
2 large onions, finely sliced
2 tsp ginger, garlic and chilli paste
8 curry leaves
1 lb cubed lean lamb or beef
6 fl oz thick coconut milk (p. 7)
8oz canned chopped tomatoes

In a small bowl, mix the first 4 ingredients with 6 tablespoons water to a smooth paste. Heat the oil in a heavy pan and fry the onions until golden brown. Add the ginger, garlic and chilli paste, curry leaves and the spice paste and fry until the oil rises above the *masala*. Add the meat and fry until evenly sealed. Lower the heat, cover the pan and simmer for about 45 minutes. Add the coconut milk and tomatoes and mix well. Simmer gently until the meat is fully cooked. Serve hot with plain rice.

Gosht Surmahi

Lamb with Fenugreek Leaves

The Kolhapuri people's food is rich, heavy in meat and full of red Sankeshwari chillies. Their ingenuity in cooking meat in a variety of pungent gravies is legendary and, although the palaces are now empty, the food has a nostalgic royal air about it.

---

2 lb spring lamb, cubed
5 green cardamoms
2 black cardamoms
2 in piece cinnamon stick
4 bay leaves
Purée:
2oz fresh ginger
6 cloves garlic
2 medium-size onions
10 fresh red chillies
14oz canned chopped tomatoes
4oz kasoori methi (*dried fenugreek leaves*)
salt to taste

Place the lamb, cardamoms, cinnamon, and bay leaves in a heavy pan and cover with cold water. Bring to a boil and simmer until the water has nearly evaporated, skimming any froth if necessary. Fold in the remaining ingredients and gently cook until the lamb is fully cooked and the gravy thick, about 1 1/2 hours.

Buhari Gosht

Madras-style Meat

Being locked up in a convent in Madras with only a twice yearly "day pass" meant that our first destination outside was a Buhari restaurant. The Muslim chef from Southern India prepared this delicious *gosht* and let us eat as much as we could, with unlimited boiled rice.

---

4 tbsp vegetable oil
1 large onion, finely sliced
4 each of cloves and green cardamoms
4 each of fresh green and dry red chillies, chopped
1 tsp turmeric powder
4 tbsp bhuna masala
1 lb lamb chops
14oz canned chopped tomatoes
salt to taste and a pinch of sugar
fresh coriander, chopped

Heat the oil in a heavy pan and fry the onion, cloves, cardamoms and chillies until the onions are brown. Add the turmeric, *bhuna masala,* and chops. Sauté until all the chops are evenly sealed. Cover the pan and simmer on a very low heat for about 10 minutes. Add the remaining ingredients, reserving a little of the coriander for garnish. Cook until the chops are fully done. Garnish and serve hot. If you wish, sprinkle a little lemon juice over the meat.

Galina Xacutti

Goan Chicken

It is difficult, with just one recipe, to lead you into the sanctum of Goan (now Panjim) cuisine. The method of eating is both a meal and a ritual. The local men start drinking *feni*, a potent cashew liquor, in the afternoon to set the pace and mood for the pungent and spicy food that follows.

1/2 cup desiccated coconut	2 onions, finely sliced
2 tsp each cumin, coriander, and mustard seeds	I tsp turmeric
	salt to taste and a pinch of sugar
4 cloves garlic and I in fresh ginger	3 lb chicken, skinned and jointed
4 cloves and 8 peppercorns	9 fl oz thick coconut milk
6 whole dry red chillies	
I tsp five-spice powder	4 tbsp tomato purée
I onion, chopped	I tsp nutmeg, freshly-grated
4 tbsp oil	

Dry-roast the coconut, spices, garlic, ginger, peppercorns, cloves, chillies, and onion in a frying pan until the onion and desiccated coconut are a deep golden brown. Grind all of these in a processor to a smooth paste and reserve. Heat the oil and fry the sliced onions until brown. Add the *masala* paste, turmeric, and salt. Fry for 2–3 minutes. Add the chicken and remaining ingredients. Bring to a boil, then simmer until the chicken is cooked and the gravy is thick.

Mulligatawny

Anglo-Indian Stew

An Indian miniature Amsterdam, Cochin is a complex of islands
and towns linked by bridges and ferries influenced by the past
— Dutch — and the present. Originally called *mulla-ga-tani*, this
dish was diversified with addition of meats, coconut milk and
tomatoes, through the Dutch influence.

I pt chicken or vegetable stock
I onion, finely chopped
8 oz fresh or canned tomatoes, chopped
I tsp each garlic and ginger paste
2 in cinnamon stick
6–8 curry leaves
I tsp each coriander and cumin powder
$^{1}/_{2}$ tsp fenugreek powder or 8–10 fenugreek seeds
9 fl oz thick coconut milk
3 lb boned chicken pieces or
2 lb raw king prawns, shelled and deveined
I onion, finely sliced and deep-fried
4 tbsp lemon juice
salt to taste
a handful of fresh coriander leaves, chopped

Place the first 10 ingredients in a large pan and bring to a boil.
Simmer for about 10 minutes. Add the chicken or prawns and
simmer until they are cooked (about $^{1}/_{2}$ hour for chicken, and
until prawns turn pink; prawns require less cooking time). Fold
in the remaining ingredients and serve hot.

Murgh Char Minar

Chicken from the Four Minarets

Hyderabad, my home town, has a rich and varied three-hundred-year-old history during which the Mughlai and Andhra menus have jostled side by side in unparalleled exotica. This merging of cultures is unmatched anywhere else in India.

---

1 tbsp vegetable oil
8oz onion, finely chopped
2oz each fresh chopped ginger and garlic paste
8oz lean ground lamb or beef
1 tbsp green masala
7 fl oz yogurt
4 hard-boiled eggs, coarsely chopped
4oz blanched flaked almonds
2 tsp salt
3 lb oven-ready chicken
1 sachet powdered saffron

Heat the oil on medium heat and fry the onions, ginger and garlic until the onions are translucent. Add the ground meat, green *masala* and half the yogurt and mix well. Cook until the meat is half done. Remove from heat. Fold in the chopped eggs, half the flaked almond, and 1 tsp salt. Stuff this mixture inside the chicken and tie or skewer the openings. Mix the remaining yogurt with the saffron and spread over the outside of the chicken. Sprinkle with the remaining salt. Roast in a preheated oven at 350°F, allowing 15—20 minutes per pound. Rest chicken for 5 minutes before carving. Serve hot, garnished with the remaining almonds and a crisp green salad.

Murgh Tikka Masala

Chicken Kebabs with Sauce

The cuisine of the Punjab is known for being rich in protein and fats — both of which are necessary to keep the Punjabi temperament going at full steam. Punjabi cooking has been to concoct mouthwatering dishes many of which have reached the west, gaining immediate popularity.

---

4 tbsp tikka masala
4 oz natural yogurt
salt to taste
I tsp sugar
4 chicken breasts, skinned, boned and cubed
Sauce:
2 tbsp tikka masala
4 oz natural yogurt
3 fl oz heavy cream
I tsp sugar
juices collected in grill tray

Mix the first 4 ingredients and marinade the chicken for I hour, or longer if possible. Grill under medium heat, resting chicken on a mesh grid or on skewers. Baste and turn the chicken pieces over and grill until well-cooked. Keep hot. To make the sauce, mix all the ingredients in a small pan. Gently heat, stirring constantly to avoid curdling. When the sauce is smooth, the oil will float. Adjust seasoning if necessary. Pour over chicken and serve with rice or *naan* (p. 8) and a green salad.

Murgh ka Salan

Bhori-style Chicken

Festive Muslim *bhori* dinners are served on the floor on a *dastar khan* — a white linen cloth which has been delicately decorated with raw grains, flower petals and greenery. When the meal is over, all of the decorations are thrown into a river, lake or well.

4 tbsp vegetable oil	3 lb chicken (remove
2 medium onions, finely sliced	skin and bone if you wish)
1 tsp garam masala	2 tbsp tomato purée
4 tsp bhuna masala	9 fl oz canned tomatoes
1 tsp turmeric powder	6 fl oz thick
5 fl oz water	coconut milk
	salt to taste

Heat the oil and fry the onions until golden brown. In the meantime mix the *masalas* and turmeric with the water. When the onions are brown add the *masalas* and fry for 3—5 minutes. Add the chicken and fry until evenly browned. Add the remaining ingredients, mix well, lower the heat and simmer covered until the chicken is done. Serve hot. (Fold in ¹/₂ tsp sugar if you wish before serving.)

Dhansak

Hot, Sweet, and Sour Potpourri

Parsis came to India from Persia bringing their own culinary genius. A reporter found a young student who read the newspaper marriage columns and thereby attended 150 Parsi feasts during his 3 years at university in Bombay.

2oz each red gram (tuwar), Bengal gram (channa)
green gram (moong) and red lentils (masoor)
4 fresh mint leaves or $^1/_2$ tsp mint sauce
12 fl oz water
1 large egg plant, potato and carrot
4oz deep-fried onions
1 oz dried fenugreek leaves
4 tbsp vegetable oil
3 tsp each of ginger, garlic, green chilli paste
3 tbsp dhansak masala
4oz fresh coriander, chopped
1 lb chicken portions or raw king prawns
4 tbsp lemon juice
salt to taste and 1 tsp sugar

Place the first 6 items in a heavy pan and bring to a boil. Simmer until the lentils and vegetables are soft and can be mashed with a wooden spoon. Reserve. In a separate pan, heat the oil and fry the spices and *masala*, coriander and chicken pieces. When the chicken pieces are sealed, add the lentil and vegetable sauce and simmer until the chicken is cooked. Add the lemon juice and seasoning and serve hot with *Baghara Khushka* (p. 8). If you use prawns, reduce the cooking time.

Porcheri

South Indian Vegetable Stew

Udipi, Vihar, and Bhavan are generic names for Southern Indian vegetarian restaurants. Food is served on banana leaves and, as you unfold the banana leaf and get ready to eat, remember to sprinkle your leaf with water from the glass already set out. The waiter will not serve you until this cleansing ritual has been completed.

8oz Bengal gram (channa dhal)
1 lb cut mixed vegetables of your choice
1 1/2 tsp chilli powder
1 tsp turmeric powder
salt to taste
2 tsp soft brown sugar
8oz desiccated coconut
4 tbsp coconut or vegetable oil
1 tsp each mustard and cumin seeds
6–8 curry leaves

Well cover and cook the *dhal* with water until soft. Drain and reserve the water. Gently mash the *dhal* with a wooden spoon and keep aside. Cook the vegetables in the reserved water with chilli and turmeric powder, salt, sugar, and half the coconut. When the vegetables are done add the *dhal* and gently fold together. Heat the oil and fry the seeds, curry leaves, and remaining coconut until the coconut is light brown. Pour all this over the vegetable and *dhal* and mix well. Reheat the whole mixture and serve hot.

Gucci Mattar Paneer

Mushroom, Peas, and Cheese Curry

In Rajasthan *Teej Mala* (Festival of Devi) is essentially for women and in particular mothers and their daughters-in-law. Devi, the wife of Lard Shiva, is worshipped for two days to obtain her gratitude. Only vegetarian dishes are cooked by the daughters-in-law to remain in the grace and favor of the mothers-in-law. Feta can be used as a substitute for *paneer*.

Purée:	4 tbsp ghee *or vegetable oil*
8oz canned tomatoes	*l tsp nigella seeds* (ajwain)
l tsp each ginger and garlic paste	*8oz button mushrooms, halved*
6 green chillies	*8oz garden peas*
l tsp pasanda masala	*8oz paneer, cubed and fried until golden*
6 fl oz heavy cream	
¹/2 tsp cornstarch	*handful of fresh coriander leaves, chopped*
l small onion	

Heat the *ghee* or oil and fry the nigella seeds. Add the puréed *masala* and sauté over medium heat stirring constantly. Fold in the mushrooms, peas and *paneer*. Simmer for 15 minutes. Garnish with the coriander leaves and serve hot.

Dahi-ni-Kari

Yogurt Curry

Masters of vegetarian cooking, Gujeratis make, in an endless procession, a variety of mouth-watering dishes from the simplest lentils and vegetables.

12oz yogurt, beaten
4 fl oz thin coconut milk
4 tbsp gram flour (p. 7) mixed in ½ cup water
½ tsp each turmeric and chilli powder
salt to taste and ½ tsp sugar
10oz corn kernels with peppers
4 tbsp vegetable oil
4 whole dried red chillies
1 tsp cumin seeds
2 cloves garlic, crushed
6–8 curry leaves
¼ tsp asafoetida

Mix the yogurt, coconut milk, flour, turmeric, chilli powder, salt and sugar and pass through a sieve. Add corn and peppers and over a low heat simmer the mixture until the sauce is smooth and thick. Set aside. Heat the oil and fry the remaining ingredients until the garlic turns golden brown. Pour the oil and spices over the yogurt sauce and cover the pan to infuse. Gently reheat and serve plain or compliment with *Bhajias* (p. 43). If you are adding the *Bhajias* allow them to simmer in the curry for 5 minutes before serving.

Ande aur Tamatar ka Cut

Egg and Tomato Curry

This dish originated in the Deccan and the *Dakhnis* love their food hot. Traditionally served with *Biryani* (p. 11), you can add vegetables of your choice to make an even more wholesome dish.

---

1 1/2 pts tomato juice
2oz coconut cream
4 tbsp gram flour (besan) mixed in a little water
2 tsp kashmiri masala
1 tsp garam masala
salt to taste and 1/2 tsp sugar
2 tsp each vegetable oil and sesame oil
1 tsp cumin seeds
4 whole dried red chillies
6 curry leaves
4 cloves garlic, sliced
1/4 tsp asafoetida
4 hard-boiled eggs, halved
browned onions and fresh coriander for garnish

Mix the first 6 items in a large pan and gently heat until the coconut has dissolved. In a frying pan heat the oils and fry the remaining ingredients except the eggs and garnish. When the garlic slices are a deep golden brown pour everything over the tomato mixture and cover to allow the spice aroma to infuse. Reheat gently, float the halved eggs on top and garnish with browned onions and coriander and serve hot.

Bhajias

Savory Fritters

At Navratri, the festival of Nine Nights during which Durga, the warrior goddess, is worshipped, people only eat light snacks like *bhajias, samosas, pakoras,* etc. India seems to have more snacks than any other country in the world.

---

*8oz gram flour (*besan *or* channa atta*)*
I tsp baking powder
salt to taste
½ tsp each turmeric and chilli powder
½ tsp each onion, nigella, cumin and fennel seeds, coarsely ground
2 green chillies, finely chopped
handful of fresh coriander leaves, chopped
2 large onions, finely sliced

Sift the flour, baking powder, salt, turmeric, and chilli powder together in a large mixing bowl. Add the remaining ingredients and toss. Gradually add water and, using your hand, mix the ingredients in until you have a thick consistency batter. Heat sufficient oil for deep-frying and, when smoking hot, drop spoonfuls of the mixture and fry until golden brown. Drain well and serve or use in *Dahi-ni-Kari* (p. 39).

Ringanano Olo

Stuffed Egg Plant

Sun and sand color the lives of the Kutch, people whose lifestyle is very much a result of their desert environment. The cuisine is innovative through necessity and vegetable dishes are available only when the vegetable supply comes in from neighboring states.

---

2 large deep-purple egg plant	I tsp chilli powder
4 tbsp vegetable oil	I tsp each turmeric and
I tsp each mustard and	coriander powder
cumin seeds	salt to taste
8oz spring onions,	$^1/_2$ tsp sugar
finely chopped	

Wash and wipe the egg plant without trimming the tails. Using I teaspoon oil rub the egg plant all over and bake in a moderately hot oven at 350°F until the skins blacken. Remove, but leave the oven on a low setting. When the egg plant are cool to handle cut in half and scoop out the white pulp. Return the cases on a greased tray to the oven. Mash the pulp coarsely and reserve. Heat the remaining oil and fry the seeds and spring onions for 2—3 minutes. Add the remaining ingredients and the mashed pulp. Mix well. Refill the egg plant cases with the spiced pulp and return to the oven for about 20 minutes. This can also be served as a starter garnished with lemon wedges.

Tarka Dhal

Lentils Seasoned with Hot Oil and Spices

Rice and *dhal* are the mainsprings of the working man's diet. In Varanasi, one of India's oldest cities, the god Ganesh is worshipped and special foods prepared from the new harvest for a feast. Later, clay images of the god are immersed into the Ganga River and sand from the river bed is sprinkled around the grain stores for his blessing.

I cup mixed red grain lentils (masoor and tuwar)
3 cups water
¹/₂ tsp turmeric powder
2 whole green chillies, stems removed
I tsp salt
Seasoning (final fry):
4 tbsp vegetable oil
I onion, finely sliced
2 cloves garlic, finely sliced
¹/₂ tsp each of mustard, onion and cumin seeds
6 curry leaves
2 whole dry red chillies
I tsp lemon juice and a few fresh coriander leaves

Pick and wash the *dhals* and drain. Place the first 4 ingredients in a pot and bring to a boil. Lower the heat and simmer with the pot half covered until the *dhals* are soft and most of the water has evaporated. Add salt and mash the *dhals* with a wooden spoon, adjusting the consistency with boiling water, if too thick. Transfer to an ovenproof serving dish and keep warm. In a small frying pan heat the oil and fry the onion and garlic until golden brown. Add the seeds, curry leaves and red chillies and fry for 2—3 minutes. Pour all this over the *dhals*. Sprinkle with lemon juice and coriander leaves and serve.

Patra ni Macchi

Stuffed Fish Rolls

This is a famous Parsi dish traditionally baked in banana leaves. Like the English Sunday roast this is prepared on Sundays and served along with *Dhansak* (p. 32).

---

4 fillets of Dover, lemon sole or plaice (if your fish market is friendly, request the white fillets)
a batch of Kotmir Pudina *chutney (p. 35)*
salt to taste
4 pieces (10 in x 10 in) special plastic wrap for cooking
wedges of lemon or lime

Wash and dry the fish fillets. Rub the flesh side generously with the chutney and sprinkle salt to taste. Roll the fillets and wrap each in a piece of the plastic wrap and tie the ends together. Drop the rolls into boiling water and cook for 10—15 minutes. Remove and when cool enough to handle remove the plastic wrap. Serve each person a roll or cut them into slices to look like "swiss-roll" slices. Serve with lemon or lime wedges.

Sarson Jingha

Mustard Spinach with Prawns

The sea-kissed town of Konarak in the state of Orissa is a popular tourist resort. Oriya cuisine depends on seafood and is liberally spiced with mustard — an influence from West Bengal — yet the food has a delectable difference.

---

1 lb raw king prawns, shelled and deveined
1 tsp turmeric
salt to taste
4 tsp mustard or vegetable oil
1/4 tsp onion seeds (kalonji)
6–8 curry leaves
2 tsp pasanda masala
15oz canned mustard spinach (sarson)
2 large tomatoes, chopped
handful of fresh coriander leaves

Rub the prawns with the turmeric and salt and keep aside. Heat the oil on medium heat and fry the onion seeds, curry leaves and green *masala* for 2–3 minutes. Add the prawns and stir-fry until they are bright orange in color. Fold in the mustard spinach, tomatoes and coriander leaves. Heat to serving temperature and serve with rice or bread.

Xevttallo Molee

Salmon with Chilli-Coconut Sauce

When fresh coconut, chillies, and the Manglorean mind fuse, the result is pure culinary magic! Gleaned from the traditional repertoire of this coastal region, here is a classic recipe which displays the ingenuity of yet another genre of Indian cuisine.

I tsp cumin powder
1 1/2 tsp chilli powder, or to taste
1/2 tsp turmeric powder
I tbsp wine vinegar
1 1/2 tsp slat or to taste
4–6oz salmon steaks or fillets
4 tbsp vegetable oil
1 3/4 cups thick coconut milk (p. 7)
Purée:
I large onion
6 green chillies
4 cloves garlic
4 in piece fresh ginger
1 1/2 tsp each cumin and coriander powder

Mix the first 5 ingredients into a paste. Coat the salmon thoroughly and marinade for 30 minutes. Heat the oil and fry the puréed ingredients for 5 minutes on medium heat. Add the coconut milk and bring the sauce to a boil. Reduce the heat and gently slip in the salmon. Cook each side in the sauce for 5–8 minutes. Arrange the salmon on a warmed plate and spoon the sauce around them and serve with lemon wedges.

Kotmir Pudina Chutney

Coriander and Mint Relish

An entire book could be written on the chutneys and pickles of India. This has always been my favorite and can be used in many different ways; an accompaniment to any curry or sandwich, or mixed with natural yogurt as a variation to *raitha* (p. 12) or fish filling.

---

2 tbsp vegetable oil
2oz desiccated coconut
2 green chillies and 2 dried red chillies
$^1/_2$ tsp each mustard, cumin, fennel and onion seeds
4 curry leaves
4oz fresh coriander washed and drained
4 tbsp lemon juice
2 tsp mint sauce
salt to taste and I tsp sugar

Heat the oil and fry the coconut, chillies, seeds, and curry leaves until the coconut is golden brown. Cool the mixture and place in a food processor along with the remaining ingredients. Blend until the coriander is finely chopped. Adjust seasoning and lemon juice if necessary. Serve cold.

Aamba Piyali

Mango Cups

Mango is a very sacred fruit in India. It is said that Lord Shiva brought the mango tree from heaven for his beautiful wife Parvathi whose favorite fruit it was and who had become very upset when she found that mango was not available on earth. Alfonso, Rasdhara, Malgoba, and Neelam are some of the Indian mangoes available abroad between April and July from Indian grocers.

---

2 ripe mangoes
4 tsp sugar
1 sachet saffron powder
4 tbsp heavy cream

Wash the mangoes and dry them gently. Make a cut right through to the seed around the center of each mango. Hold each mango on both sides of the cut and twist carefully. Two halves will be like cups and the other two will have the seed sticking out. Carefully remove the seeds. Scoop out the inside flesh without damaging the skins. Mash the flesh coarsely and mix in the remaining ingredients. Refill the mango cups with this mixture, chill well, and serve. This is very refreshing after a spicy meal.

Shrikhand

Yogurt and Cheese Dessert

Gokulashtmi, the birthday of the Lord Krishna, is celebrated in honour of his childhood pranks. Earthen pots containing yogurt, cream and money are suspended from a huge rope on every street corner. Groups of young boys and men climb on each other's shoulders to form a human pyramid to reach and break the pots.

---

¹/₂ cup yogurt
8oz half-fat cheese
2oz full-fat cheese
2–4oz confectioners' sugar
¹/₂ tsp each ground cardamom and nutmeg
8–10 strands saffron or 1 sachet of powdered saffron
almond flakes and pink rose petals to garnish

Chill a large mixing bowl in the refrigerator for 1 hour. Place the cheese and yogurt in the bowl and whisk until evenly mixed. Gradually add the sugar and keep whisking until you have a light and creamy mixture. Taste as you add the sugar. You may not wish to use all of it. Add the cardamom, nutmeg and saffron and mix again. Decorate with the almond flakes and petals, chill and serve.

Index